The Songwriter's
POCKET NOTEBOOK

Writer and Editor
James Strange
BSc (Hons), PGCE

Copyright © 2025 by Penny Music Co

Originally published by Penny Music Co in 2021

A division of Dragonfly Publishing Group Ltd

Registered Office: The Octagon, Craigencalt Farm, Kinghorn, Burntisland, Fife, Scotland, KY3 9YG

Registered in Scotland No. 779822

All rights reserved. International copyright secured.

No part of this publication may be copied, reproduced, stored in a retrieval system, or transmitted in any form or by any means—electronic, mechanical, photocopying, recording, or otherwise—without prior written permission from the publisher.

Unauthorised reproduction of this material is a violation of applicable laws and may result in legal action.

ISBN: 9781738417766

www.pennymusicco.org · enquiries@pennymusicco.org

HOW TO USE THIS BOOK....

This log book is designed to encourage you to spill your musical ideas on to the page, using our song writing tips.

Jot down that melody the minute it comes to you, write those lyrics you've been repeating in your head for weeks.

Filled with pages for both lyrics and musical notation, you will be able to organise your musical inspirations like never before...

WITHOUT BEING EITHER DRAWING OR WRITING, MUSIC PARTAKES OF THE NATURE OF BOTH...

SONG WRITING TIPS...

1. Start with the title.
Jot down some memorable words or phrases and put together a title which is emotive to you. Try to use imagery or an action word to give your title some punch. Starting with a title will help you stay focused on a single idea.

2. Use the title to make a list of questions.
Think about why you chose this title and what your listeners will want to know. Your list could include questions such as: What inspired this title? How does it make you feel? What happens next?

3. Choose a song structure.
The most common structures are verse-chorus-verse-chorus-bridge-chorus. The chorus will often have more energy than the verse, and a bridge may use a change of key or altered chord progression to add anticipation for the final chorus.

4. Pick one question to answer in the chorus and one for each verse.
Focus on the chorus first, as it's usually the catchy part of the song, and select one of your questions to answer. Write down a short answer using verbs and adjectives to describe mood/colour/warmth. What is the singer thinking?

SONG WRITING TIPS (CONT.)...

5. Find the melody in your lyric.
This next bit is fun... choose one of the phrases you came up with in step 4 and say it out loud. Really listen to the rhythm of the words and accentuate the natural melody as you speak. Give it some emotion and play around with the 'feel' until it *feels* comfortable.

6. Add some chords over your chorus melody.
Play around with simple chord progressions until you find something you like, and that fits your melody. Chords I-IV-V and VI work well as a solid foundation (e.g., C-F-G and A), and can be made infinitely more interesting by starting your melodic phrases *between* chord changes.

7. Work on the lyric in your first verse.
Remember those questions in step 4? It's time to answer the one you chose for your first verse. As this is the opening line of the song, you want it to be interesting and keep the listener interested. Try restating the first line in the second line, don't move on too quickly as you need to give your listener time to understand what is happening in the song. Repeat steps 5 and 6 with your verse melody.

8. Connect your verse and chorus.
Make the transition between your verse and chorus as smooth as possible. You may need to adapt the melody slightly to move from one to the other in a natural manner. For example, the chorus is usually higher than the verse as it tends to be more emotional.

SONG WRITING TIPS (CONT.)...

9. Build your second verse and bridge.

It's time to answer the second question you asked for your second verse (your second chorus is a repeat of the first chorus). Use step 7 to help build your second verse. The good news is you have nearly written your song!

If you want to add extra strength, a bridge is a good call. It should be about three lines of vocals, with a different melody to the verse and chorus. The bridge gives the most insight into what the song is *actually* about ...like a big reveal!

10. Record your song.

Put it all together and have a go at recording yourself singing and playing the melody. It's sometimes easier to record these parts separately to give the most attention to the expression of the lyrics. Listen back, and experiment until you find the right sound.

Song No.1
NOTES

"Musicians want to be the loud voice for so many quiet hearts."

– Billy Joel

SONG TITLE

....

WHAT QUESTIONS COULD YOU ASK ABOUT THIS TITLE?

WHAT IS THE SONG'S STRUCTURE?

....

....

....

....

....

....

OR JUST SKETCH IT OUT...

USE THIS PAGE TO JOT DOWN ANY WORDS OR PHRASES YOU FIND INSPIRING OR EMOTIONAL...

Song Ideas

Song No.2
NOTES

"The wise musicians are those who play what they can master."

– Duke Ellington

SONG TITLE

....

WHAT QUESTIONS COULD YOU ASK ABOUT THIS TITLE?

WHAT IS THE SONG'S STRUCTURE?

....
....
....
....
....
....

OR JUST SKETCH IT OUT...

USE THIS PAGE TO JOT DOWN ANY WORDS OR PHRASES YOU FIND INSPIRING OR EMOTIONAL...

Song No.3
NOTES

"Be your own artist, and always be confident in what you're doing.
If you're not going to be confident, you might as well not be doing it."

- Aretha Franklin

SONG TITLE

....

WHAT QUESTIONS COULD YOU ASK ABOUT THIS TITLE?

WHAT IS THE SONG'S STRUCTURE?

....
....
....
....
....
....

OR JUST SKETCH IT OUT...

USE THIS PAGE TO JOT DOWN ANY WORDS OR PHRASES YOU FIND INSPIRING OR EMOTIONAL...

Song Ideas

Song No.4
NOTES

"Musicians don't retire; they stop when there's no more music in them."

– Louis Armstrong

SONG TITLE

....

WHAT QUESTIONS COULD YOU ASK ABOUT THIS TITLE?

WHAT IS THE SONG'S STRUCTURE?

....

....

....

....

....

....

OR JUST SKETCH IT OUT...

USE THIS PAGE TO JOT DOWN ANY WORDS OR PHRASES YOU FIND INSPIRING OR EMOTIONAL...

Song No.5
NOTES

"A musician should only sound like what they do, and no two musicians sound the same.
It's an individual-feel thing, you know?"

- Dave Grohl

SONG TITLE

....

WHAT QUESTIONS COULD YOU ASK ABOUT THIS TITLE?

WHAT IS THE SONG'S STRUCTURE?

....
....
....
....
....
....

OR JUST SKETCH IT OUT...

USE THIS PAGE TO JOT DOWN ANY WORDS OR PHRASES YOU FIND INSPIRING OR EMOTIONAL...

Song Ideas

Song No.6
NOTES

"If everything was perfect, you would never learn and you would never grow."

– Beyoncé

SONG TITLE

....

WHAT QUESTIONS COULD YOU ASK ABOUT THIS TITLE?

WHAT IS THE SONG'S STRUCTURE?

OR JUST SKETCH IT OUT...

USE THIS PAGE TO JOT DOWN ANY WORDS OR PHRASES YOU FIND INSPIRING OR EMOTIONAL...

Song No. 7
NOTES

"Despite everything, no one can dictate who you are to other people."

– Prince

SONG TITLE

....

WHAT QUESTIONS COULD YOU ASK ABOUT THIS TITLE?

WHAT IS THE SONG'S STRUCTURE?

....
....
....
....
....
....

OR JUST SKETCH IT OUT...

USE THIS PAGE TO JOT DOWN ANY WORDS OR PHRASES YOU FIND INSPIRING OR EMOTIONAL...

Song Ideas

Song No.8
NOTES

"I believe musicians have a duty, a responsibility to reach out, to share your love or pain with others."

– James Taylor

SONG TITLE

....

WHAT QUESTIONS COULD YOU ASK ABOUT THIS TITLE?

WHAT IS THE SONG'S STRUCTURE?

....
....
....
....
....
....

OR JUST SKETCH IT OUT...

USE THIS PAGE TO JOT DOWN ANY WORDS OR PHRASES YOU FIND INSPIRING OR EMOTIONAL...

Song Ideas

"The true beauty of music is that it connects people.
It carries a message, and we, the musicians, are the messengers."

- Roy Ayers

www.ingramcontent.com/pod-product-compliance
Lightning Source LLC
Chambersburg PA
CBHW030232100526
44583CB00013BA/971